Family Secrets

I0176533

by
Nadja

NadjaMedia.com

Nadja Media
530 Los Angeles Ave., Suite 115
Moorpark, California 93021

ISBN 10: 1-942057-08-3
ISBN13: 978-1-942057-08-6

The author is not a medical doctor and does not give medical advice. If you are having emotional problems you need to consult with a medical professional or a certified counselor. Nadja never advocates the use of violence in any form.

Dedication

This book is made available to inspire others from similar backgrounds to heal. There is light at the end of the tunnel. Giving voice to all those who kept it inside. This book would fit in with 12-Step programs and with people in Recovery.

— Nadja

Acknowledgments

Speaking your truth will set you free.

Poetry therapy works wonders.

Introduction

This writing chronicles a deeply personal journey from growing up in a severely dysfunctional family to attaining emotional freedom and health through healing, forgiveness, and hard inner work. The writing can give hope to those from a similar background. It is poetry therapy at its best and may inspire others to heal their past by writing similar work.

Contents

Family Secrets

By

Nadja

Lessons I Learned From My Father

My father taught me very well

He took me to the depths of Hell

I hated him with such passionate intensity

Like napalm that was plastered

And stuck on me

Burning up my heart and gut

Burning and burning and burning them up

With a hatred so powerful and great

It revealed and sealed my self-created fate

For years upon years I could not relate

To anyone who passed my gate

I was like a dangerous viper

A sniper hissing in my piss

If anyone dared to touch me

I would strike out and rarely miss

Leaving dead bodies in my path

Deaf to their screams in my wrath

It all started with terror

Which turned to hate

Until I refused

To participate

A female monster running loose

With anger and rage

Fit like a noose

Around my neck

Let the world go to heck

This took me to the point in life

Where I was filled with

So much strife

I could not stand anyone

But I hated primarily men

And swore I would kill

Every friggin' last one of them

My scars were like

Badges worn

There's nothing like

A woman's scorn

So riveted was

My attention on my father

I became entirely him

No longer his daughter

What you hate

You become

A very tough lesson

But worth a ton

Yes, he had a brilliant mind

But no soul

That I could find

He had a brilliant mind

That's true

But sick and evil

Through and through

My house was like Auschwitz

Filled with insane laughter,

Gut wrenching sobs,

Screams, and fits

Beating frenzies

Hatred, cursing

Uncontrolled rages

Tons of hurting

Kick the dog

Rape your wife

Threaten to kill her

With your knife

Family secrets

Under threat to tell

Isolate, damage

And create more hell

From outside

Our family looked good

Inside there were continuous attacks

Upon our personhood

Which none of us

Ever really understood

The atmosphere

Was fraught with danger

With thoughts of murder

I was no stranger

My crazy insane home

Was the perfect birthing place

For Post Traumatic

Stress Syndrome

This was the filter

Through which I saw the world

As my unusual, drama-filled

Life unfurled

Is it any wonder

That I married a violent man

Who abused me daily

And almost put me under

We often marry our parents

To help us heal

From the wounds and the pain

That we carry and feel

Many times I thought

If reincarnation's true

I must have been a hellion

Evil through and through

To have been born

At that place in time

To a father who was insanely crazy

And never ever kind

Thank God I did not die

Or take my life

For now in my latter years

I no longer have any strife

No more searing hot tears

Through miracles, forgiveness

And hard, grueling Work

I've become

A loving Human Being

No longer a jerk

No more pity parties

No, not for me

The Veil has been lifted

I now can truly See

How beautiful and tender

Life can be

Look what I missed

Through all of those years

Of ignorance, arrogance,

And self-centered tears

I do not want to waste

One more minute

Living the life

That was intended for me

In freedom and love

Touched from Above

So very tenderly

I've forgiven my father

He was a most unfortunate soul

He died in extreme anguish

Never surrendering or letting go

The pain he lived with

Was inflicted on us

We had open sores on our souls

Filled with his pus

Wherever he is

I hope he's at rest

For in his twisted mind

He did what he thought best

(I guess)

I just started to live

Late in life

And who knows

I may even choose

To become a wife

To sleep with my former enemy

But now with love

And Grace from above

No more, any more enmity

This is indeed

A tale of woe

But the ending is sweet

I'm good to go

How I survived, I do not know

Hatred is a horrible bedfellow

It will take you down

And in its grip you will drown

I know hatred through and through

I know just what it can do

It will destroy your soul

And extinguish you

I am now healed

As this long piece has revealed

If my life would end today

''Thank You, Thank You,''

Is all that I could say

For this magnificent Life

It is a Gift

No longer am I

Completely adrift

I'm anchored here

Warrior strong

Ready for anything

That comes along

I've now got a healthy

Mind and soul

Just let it all rip

Let it all roll

To have survived it all

And come out the other end

Is an absolute miracle

To which I say,

"Amen, Amen, and Amen," again.

I emerged with

Great strength and resilience

A loving, kind heart

To buffer my brilliance

And so at last I can say

It was a wild, tumultuous ride

All the way from birth

Until this very day

From where I sit right now

I wouldn't have changed a thing

For this life I've lived

Has come full circle

And all I want to do is sing

Sing songs of love

With such excruciating beauty

That they will melt the hearts of those

Stuck in the nightmare of duty

To bring them to Know

That they too can grow

Out of the pain they did endure

To become a healed soul and pure

Pure in the spirit that is

Singing their own true song

Of their travails on Earth

And how they've come along

To at last

Know who they are

A Magnificent Being

Birthed from a Star

I'm no longer

Afraid of what I'll do

I'm totally healed and safe

No harm ever to you

When we reach out

To where we're all connected

All we want to do

Is to heal souls

Who were similarly affected

Like we were, tortured

Within the sanctity of our home

Feeling totally powerless

And completely alone

Subjected to bizarre behavior

With no one to talk to

No awakened inner knowledge

No loving savior

You can tell me, I understand,

I've been through it all

Yes, you can heal

You can once more stand tall

It is just an illusion

This Veil of Tears

It is filled with land mines

Beauty, torture, and

Ungodly fears

Some live in beauty

And are surrounded by love

They must have been saints

Sent from above

But for you and me

We were blessed with tragedy

To polish and hone us

So eventually we could See

See the beauty of Soul

From Orchestra Seats

A close-up view

It's just one of the treats

When you Wake up

To your Knowing

That all is well

Your story was the perfect tale

Given only to you to tell

About good and evil

The polarity plan

To learn your lessons

On Mother Earth's land

Wake up, Wake up

Hear yourself sing

I hear the bells

Of the Golden Age ring

We are almost there

You can feel the Light

The Shift will occur

Our future is bright

Ring out the old

Ring in the new

It's time to celebrate

The Real and Authentic You

I'm offering to show you the journey I took

As explained in detail in my book*

How I was able to transform

From an ignorant beast

To partake of the marriage feast

Not between two souls

But between the triune flame

Within our body's sacred frame

The mind, heart, and soul intertwined as one

The Battle of the Reactive Mind is done

To live our life with joy and free

Singing our Song of True Liberty

*River of Living Light

Mother

Motherhood, Motherhood

What a sacred word

Has anyone understood?

Has anyone ever heard?

A Leo with a huge ego

An injured soul

With money and prestige

As her goal

Orphaned at 12

From riches to rags

The relatives swoop in

To steal the loot

Ignoring the children

Who gives a hoot?

A second-class citizen overnight

Never fully accepted

No real love or tenderness

Nothing was really right

Living like a poor foster child

In rich relatives' homes

She was never fully included

And felt totally alone

The cousins she lived with

Were sent to college

She was ordered to work

No one paid for her knowledge

No wonder she was frozen

At the age of 12

And never recovered

But lived in hell

Married a mentally ill scientist

Who she didn't love

To create brilliant kids

Horrors kept under lids

Institutional shock treatments

Long hospital stays

While at home

The wife plays

Alliances with men

Pedophiles and such

Torture for children

Far, far too much

Kidnapping threats

Danger, danger

Police involvement

Was even stranger

This beautiful Being

My gateway to the world

Was twisted and tortured

As her life unfurled

Till death do us part

To the bitter end

Her husband died

Amen, amen

Freedom at last

But if you don't know

Who you are

You're at a loss by far

Possess the daughter

To be your slave

Total control

Serving as maid

Yes, that's correct

That's how I behaved

Daughter is chaperone

For many dates

As her mom frolics

And enjoys her mates

One day the daughter

Met a man

A drunkard scoundrel

From the battlefields

Of Vietnam

The mother entices

The man away

And really enjoys him

Her sport to play

The daughter marries him

They have a child

It's a roller coaster ride

The daughter lives in fear

Totally torn up inside

To protect self and baby

The daughter escapes

Goes to live with her mother

More hell that creates

For one another

The father was big in AA

Irresponsible and wild

Never offered a dime

To support his child

Why don't they stress

In groups like AA

To be responsible for your offspring

And have the integrity to pay?

The baby is raised

In this sick family

They struggle against the odds

These lost humans three

The daughter takes care

Of the mother and child

She is forced to the edge

The child runs wild

The mother dies

The child matures

She is now happily married

Time really cures

After years of hard work

The daughter is free

I am the daughter

The daughter is me

I am now my Authentic Self

In possession of my inner wealth

No more stress

Just time to Be

I'm a happy grandma

Who's let go of the past

I'm reinventing myself

A fulfilling life at long last

My mother was released

And taken above

She never knew peace

She never knew love

In my old age

I forgive her for all

How could she mother

Having lived bitter gall

She was the gateway

For me to enter Mother Earth

My true nurturer

Since the day of my birth

It took me forever

To process all this

I am melting with love

As I blow her a kiss

Wherever she is

In this Great Universe

I love you, Mother

For better or worse

You went through hell

And so did I

But we're both released

I want to cry

Tears of joy

Released at last

We are no longer held

Or defined by our past

I look forward

To seeing you

For now I know

As above so below

Thank you, Mom

For all your hard work

It was so difficult for you

You were terribly hurt

My heart is filled

With love for you

May your voyage in Eternity

Be blessed with the joys

You never knew

Brother

My brother was born first

And received the worst

Joining an unfortunate family

Which was blind

And could not see

His father was a maniac

Tortured and twisted

Tried to strangle his sister

His mind gone wild

Since an innocent child

My brother was beaten to a pulp

Then was screamed at to shut up

Muffled tears

Uncontrolled sobs

Multiplying fears

Trust totally broken

Any love, strictly verboten

By a sick, sick man

His birth father

In this strange, strange land

What a harsh school

This Earth can be

Set up to see

If the battered and broken

Can ever break free

Will they succumb

To their drug of choice

To numb their memories

And quiet their voice?

There is always the possibility

That they can break free

So that they can discover

Their true destiny

It's a labor of love

And hard grueling work

To untie the knots

Of all that lurks

In the psyche and mind

Hidden from view

Cutting you off

From the authentic You

The rewards are great

The cells renew

The mind clears up

Gee you are you (G-U-R-U)

We are born a full package

With everything we need

Just like a flower

Grows up from its seed

Get quiet

Sit still

Let the mind do

Whatever it will

Watch what it does

Like a movie show

Let the ticker tape play

Don't let it ruin your day

To achieve that goal

Learn how not to react

Stay calm throughout

Your mind may shout

About terrible happenings

That you want to forget

Or frightening scenes

That haven't happened yet

It may take you to places

Where you want to stay

Scenes of love

Ecstasy and play

It may beat you up

It may put you down

It may boost you to the top

Where you're wearing a crown

Whatever it says

Don't believe a word

It's just a ticker tape

Not fit to be heard

If you can remain calm

Through this movie show

You will be amazed to learn

You will be relieved to know

That the mind is an entity

It is not you

It is not a good master

It is only a tool

This tool can be used

As you want it to

Just make sure

It doesn't use you

Once you clear your mind

You can start to live

With a new perspective

And you want to give

Thanks and appreciation

For this magical life

You can now

Watch the ticker tape

Without any strife

You can enjoy this Earth

You are totally free

No worries, no hates

Wide Awake you can See

How your life unfolds

With peace and ease

No matter what happens

Life is a breeze

It's filled with joy

You're good to go

You've won the Battle

Over your strong ego

Your spirit can soar

Your spirit can fly

You can blow kisses to people

As they pass by

For now you know

That we're all one

Masquerading as personalities

Oh what great fun

To see within

Through the charade

Of smiles and pain

From the king to the maid

We're all in this together

In this Great Universe

The future will be magnificent

Throw away your purse

Money will be of no concern

We're all here

To live and to learn

To enjoy our life

With each breath

Until we change form

Through what we call death

And when we do

We leave this place

And travel and learn

In Outer and Inner Space

We just change form

We never die

We just live slices

Of the Big Pie in the Sky

From the Milky Way

To the galaxy

On to the Universe

Hey wait for me

I love a challenge

I love adventure

Let's ride the rainbow

Aloha, Buena Venture

My brother became a comedian

To hide his pain

He brings laughter to all

But what is his gain

He wonders

Where his life has gone

He never could go inward

For very long

Inward was painful

Filled with pus

Better laugh and be busy

Not examine your guts

But inward is where

The treasure lies

Do not think

It's what you see

With your eyes

Inward it is

Are you ready to look?

To find your True Self

It's not in a book

Hey, Brother,

Are you listening?

There still is time

To turn within

And explore the mine

Find the treasure within

To free your soul

So you can leave Earth

Healed and Whole

We never knew

How to treat each other

But I want you to know

I love you, Brother

We both came

From the same sick family

We were products of our environment

But, Hey I'm now free

I wish this for you

From the bottom of my heart

All is forgiven

I understand your part

How could you have

Done otherwise?

Each day your self-worth

Was reduced in size

I felt so badly

You had no choice

You were beaten down

Till you had no Voice

You turned to money

To buy you prestige

Because your childhood

Was so under siege

I guess you have learned

Now that you're old

All that glitters

Is not true gold

Hey, Brother,

Are you listening?

You have your health

Go within

And discover your wealth

I forgive you

For abandoning me

In that sick home

To set yourself free

I was actually

Happy for you

Since you were beaten down

More than you ever knew

I felt it deeply

Each hit, each curse

Each time you yelled

It made it worse

I was the favored one

You were jealous of me

But the favored one is often bought

And becomes just property

It can take forever

To break away

But, Brother, late in life

I am free today

I've cleaned out my garbage,

My cesspool

I worked hard

And did renew

I wish the very same for you

Hey, Brother, I hear you

Your inner child tells me

This is what he

Wishes you to do

Prejudicial Heritage

I am the product

Of a Nazi and a Jew

My father was the Nazi

My mother was the Jew

I discovered this by accident

At the age of 22

I was sworn to secrecy

My brother never knew

Warring factions

Within the household

Is very hard to do

But within the genetics of the body

It is torture through and through

Two diametrically opposed forces

This schizophrenic union

Took me years upon years

To unravel and undo

The other way to look at this

Is that I was totally amiss

My higher and my lower self

Would disagree and argue

I made the choice

This battle to pursue

Rather than to seek within

To heal and renew

I understand that even Hitler

Was one-quarter Jew

A fact of life that

Most the world

Never, ever knew

No doubt a psychotic, schizophrenic

Known to very few

They let him have his way

With violence and destruction

To execute bestial genocide

Without their interruption

There must be thousands out there

People just like me

Kept from knowing

The truth about their heritage

And about their family tree

This is due to ignorance and prejudice

Two dark and deadly traits

Developed out of fear and blindness

By the human race

These traits forced parents

To withhold the truth about their roots

In order to protect their children

From the vicious blind men's boots

To think that people could not be proud

Of their race or religion

Many felt the facts

Must be hidden

They were in fear for their life

If these things were known or shown

Thus their background they disowned

This forced many a person

To turn against themselves

Due to their genetics

And threats of foul eugenics

Imagine, people could not be open

About who they truly were

They could not alter the facts

But kept them quiet

In fear of the axe

I remember there was

A rabbi on the corner

That my mother knew

She visited him daily

He told her about the Jews,

The camps, and the ovens

This was during World War II

Meanwhile

My father invited his Nazi friends

"Guests" who could've peppered

The Gestapo's Who's Who

Dead to the Truth

Known to very few

That what you do to others

You actually do to you

They pretended innocence

For all they did and knew

This societal sickness is appalling

The whole system needs overhauling

Thank God the world is changing

Blinded people are now awakening

Mother Earth is even quaking

In anticipation of the day

When all separateness will go away

For we are truly One

Underneath our moon and sun

Yes, things are changing now

The Veil is being lifted

We can appreciate each other

And the heritage with which we're gifted

Maybe this great separation

Was nourishing in a way

Perhaps it was preparation

For the Awakening today

Because this practice was so bizarre

It's now obvious by far

That the damages created scars

On the whole human race

At an escalating pace

On our journey down through time

Without reason, without rhyme

And needs to be stopped and cleared

In order to go forward

So the Light can appear

Let's take down all barriers

Open our hearts as we clear all terrors

And prepare a banquet table together

To celebrate a New Day

When all the hate, fear, and misconceptions

Are at last cleared away

Yes, we are at the threshold

Of exchanging new for old

New wine for new wine skins

A time for rejoicing many fold

Something is now happening

That is hard to define

It seems we're moving rapidly

Out of the reach of time

The human race at last

Is clearing the morass

It created out of blindness

And is moving into an era

Where we all can live together

In understanding and in kindness

Perhaps the nightmare was worth it

We're now clearing up the past

The Millennium is imminent

Peace and joy will reign at last

I understand the hate

That produced the Nazi

And the fear

That branded the Jew

It's all that yin and yang

About which the sages sang

And what the mystics knew

That we are truly one

Once the dross is cleared

There is really nothing out there

Nothing to be feared

The rest is just a masquerade

For the ignorant and lost

They rape and they pillage

And rarely count the cost

They do this without knowledge

Of the workings of the mind

How the Spirit is held captive

Of people spiritually blind

They damage the world

Unknowingly hurting themselves

While destroying the fabric of life

And creating many hells

The spark of God within them

Seems dulled beyond repair

But there's hope

For the most heinous heathen

For his Creator's ever near

His treasure's buried inside of them

They know not where to look

Instead they justify their actions

By referring to some book

Unless they see the Light

Like Saul did on his path

They continue ever onward

Destructive in their wrath

May they all awake some day

To see the error of their way

Repent of all the wrongs they've done

Clearly hear the horrible song they've sung

Repent and ask forgiveness

Knowing we all are one

The Spirit being victorious

The final battle won

The Battle of the centuries

Between the many and the few

The Nazi and the Christian

The Christian and the Jew

This Battle's now resolved and over

As the mind and soul renew

To My Inner Child

Beautiful, Beloved Inner Child

How did you survive

The horrors you endured?

So thrilled you're still alive

We've had quite the journey

Others weren't so lucky

They left this world

On a lone, cold gurney

I took you places

Where you should

Never have gone

Dark, dark places

Where you didn't belong

While I visited Hell

You came along

So relieved

I didn't extinguish you

You're strong and resilient

Through and through

Things are different now

I'm wide-awake

I see with clarity

The new journey we take

From this day forth

We'll travel consciously together

Nothing can part us

Whatever comes our way

We can weather

So much time was lost

That's very sad

But let's no longer

Count the cost

We're free at last

To do as we wish

To enjoy the beauty of this world

With great relish

Let's start each day

With gratitude and love

Welcoming all the Light

Beings From here and above

Kissing the flowers

Hugging the trees

Appreciating everything

Living with ease

A fabulous journey

No stress anymore

Let's explore the world

From every forest

To every shore

I have a true companion

At long last

This wouldn't have happened

If I still lived in the past

Living moment to moment

Brings such joy

I love you, Inner Child

We have much to experience

We have much to enjoy

We can travel by day

We can travel by night, too

Through the so-called dark

Into the Light and the Indigo Blue

Let's explore the Universe

Yes, we can do this

We'll just laugh our heads off

And experience pure bliss

So sorry you had

To wait so long

For me to wake up

And come along

But what is time

In this 3rd dimension

Come along, come along

We'll experience Ascension

No more tears

No more past

The future is bright

The die is cast

We can go

Or we can be still

It's all up to us

It's as we will

Each day let's laugh

Each day let's play

Let's smile and blow kisses

To all on our way

Thank you, thank you, thank you

Is all that I can say

We're now joined together

Hip, hip hooray!

Emotions

Fear and hate were

Companions of mine

For more years than

I care to relate

Fear sears itself

Right into your being

Seemingly giving no chance

Of ever, ever freeing

Yourself from its strong grasp

Super vigilant, stone-faced

Numbed enough

To make any soul gasp

But underneath it all

A seething anger

Turned into hate

Slowly surfacing

To the point where

You can no longer relate

To anyone including you

And all you want to do

Is spew out diatribes against the world

Fight battles in the sky

Like Don Quixote

So otherworldly

That you no longer can identify

With the world as it passes by

Because you now inhabit

Castles in the sky

So distant from who you truly are

You cannot relate to anyone by far

And prefer to live alone

Your so-called soul to hone

Until you finally awake

And start to truly appreciate

The Gift that you were given

On this Planet where you're livin'

Of each magical, transformational day

When you totally get out of your way

So you can see the majesty

Of all that passes before your eyes

All that's free and supplies

Your every need, your every desire

Now that you See how things transpire

Between the world and spirit

You hear your inner voice

You really hear it

And begin to understand

The Divine Plan

That underlies it all

Despite appearances

All is well

And it's really not our call

We are on this journey together

It's a most fantastic voyage

As we travel through space

At our appointed pace

An amazing mythic story

Unfolding right before our eyes

Birthing humanity's glory

To Self-realize

It's all unfolding

Like it should

Once this epic story

Is truly understood

Of mankind transitioning from a child

To fully mature adulthood

We are so fortunate

To be here at this time

To witness the changes

That will allow us to climb

Out of the morass

Into an event so divine

The full flowering of humanity

On the Creator's magical living vine

This epic story in all its glory

Is more delicious than any wine

On gratitude and thanksgiving we will dine

The battle of the mind is won

My life just now has begun

This song I sing

Is sung for you

Wake up, wake up

Rejoice and renew

Elder Brother is coming

No, He's actually here

But He's waiting for you

To drop all your barriers

So He can at last appear

He loves you so very much

But He does not want

To be your crutch

He waits in anticipation

To unite each sovereign nation

To be the perfect birthing place

For the awakened human race

Drop your programming

Step out of the past

Step into your greatness

Awake at long last

Rape

Yes, forgive them for your sake

After they've violated you by rape

So you can live without the memories

That weigh you down

And make all men your enemies

Yes, forgive the error of the male

Who's terribly mistreated the female

Out of anger, fear, ignorance,

And powerlessness

He took it out on the beloved Goddess

How dare he and how dare we

Allow this to transpire

Taking all of us in and through the fire

Forgive them for they know not what they do

Said the Great Master to all of us

And especially to you

For this applies to us

As well as others, too

How wise He was and filled with Love

And also with equality and justice

As lived and learned Above

But the Wheels of Karma have slowly turned

The Divine Feminine's now in power

Women Awake, this is our hour

The Divine Masculine ran the world

Until they ran it into the ground

So let's look forward to this next round

As the true Goddess Energy

Is released unbound

Dear Sisters,

Let's not demand an eye for an eye

Let's heal our brothers and allow them to cry

No longer must they be in pain

And use us for their every gain

We are very capable of leading

With true power, no more pleading

But first let's heal our Brothers' wounds

They need our tender care more than ever

Our loving ties we will not sever

No more enmity between the sexes

We extend our hand in holy nexus

Let's take the helm of leadership together

To co-create a world

Where we'd like to live forever

A world that is noble and just

Fitting for the God self

That lives within each one of us

Deep in the heart of every Human Being

Let's lift the ignorance

So all of us can be seen

For who we truly are

Magnificent Beings birthed from a star

Together we can do this hand in hand

No more mistreatment upon this Sacred Land

Mother Earth, Father Sky, Brother Sun,

Great Spirit

We are ready to Listen; We are ready to hear it

We open our Hearts to You

Fill them full with Light from Above

Help us to radiate Your Love

So we can help heal our world once more

One in which Your children will flourish

Completely healed to the core

No more fear but love instead

To grace and protect

Every family's homestead

The Golden Age has just begun

The Bell of True Freedom at last has rung

John Henry Has Arrived

John Henry, John Henry

My Warrior Friend

Fighting battles

Without end

The real battlefield

Is the mind

That keeps you entrapped

That keeps you blind

It will rip you up

And shred you to bits

May you be victorious

Before you call it quits

Your heart was broken

Once before

To mend and heal it

You need to settle the score

Between your anger

And your Spirit that soars

This is the True Battle

That you must fight

To correct the wrongs

And make them right

Yes, you are a warrior strong

But do not wait

For this Great Showdown

Too long

The mind is a minefield

Filled with holes

That will break you down

Like nobody knows

Three score and ten

Is time enough It's time to mend

So mend, My Friend,

Lay down your sword

Take up the Staff

Walk strong in Spirit

Down the Warrior Path

Bitterness is a strong, strong drink

It shrivels the body

And brings you to

That precarious brink

Where you choose

Which way to go

With the mind

Or with the Flow

It's late in life

It's harvest time

Learn to enjoy it

It is so very fine

Right here and now

Beneath our nose

The Majesty of Creation

Ebbs and flows

You can partake

Lay down your gun

Release your anger

It keeps you numb

You feel your life

Just passed you by

All your effort wasted

Nothing left to do but cry

It is all an illusion

All we have is present time

So learn to live in it

No boundaries to confine

Yes, forget the past

It is dead

Rise up, rise up

Take up your bed

Live once more

In the Vibrant Light

With hope and joy

It is your birthright

Come on John Henry

Get out of your mind

Move into your heart

Your True Self to find

Cry your river of tears

About being misunderstood

And not appreciated

For your personhood

In truth your life

Has not begun

Come on, John Henry

Lay down your gun

Your child within

Is begging you

To pay it attention

But you have no clue

Find out who this is

This young innocent boy

Who was initiated with anger

And cut off from joy

Punched in the face

For seeing the truth

What a display

Of the ignorant uncouth

We've all been there

And experienced the pain

But, hey, we're still here

Still in the game

Come on, Wounded Warrior

Heal your hurt

Do the deep work

Become a convert

To the true joy of life

A life well lived

With a Spirit that's healed

And knows how to give

With no strings attached

No ego, no pity

Just a strong seasoned warrior

Travelin' city to city

To heal the land

The people and such

The Workers are needed

And needed so much

Unload your burdens

Take up the Staff

The world is waiting

To hear your True laugh

Not laughter from the mind

Filled with bitterness and blind

Not clever or cynical

No, not any of that kind

But the laughter from the heart

Overflowing with joy

John Henry has arrived

He's healed his boy

Wondrous Woman

Life lived

Heart bared

Beauty hid

Running scared

Personal demons

Chasing you

What can you

Possibly do

Try to confront them

This doesn't work

Befriend and disarm them

Meanwhile don't shirk

Your many duties in this life

Filled with hardship

Filled with strife

All that tension

All that stress

Comes to naught

When you confess

Your part in the drama

That created the mess

At last you can stand

At last you can see

To finally be able

To let it all Be

Just relax and be you

Underneath it all

Breathe deep

Stand tall

Able to love

Not in spite of

But because of it all

Universal Citizen

From little you to all in All

Your expanded Beingness

Amazingly wide and astonishingly tall

What a connection

To end the blindness

The imperfection

Always available

For those who dare

To take this path

Working through their pain and wrath

Letting go their story and past

To find their greatest treasure

Their innermost wealth and riches

Way beyond all measure

Nothing now is hidden from you

You can heal yourself and renew

See the world through new eyes

When you finally Self-realize

To at last be truly wise

For you can view all

From a heightened perspective

Become one of humanity's elected

Qualified to teach and guide

Nothing left to cover or hide

By Universal Law abide

A Global Citizen

A Galactic Being

Able to See

And be Seen

Energized by the Central Sun

Your Higher Expression has begun

Exploring your multidimensionality

Which is part and parcel

Of the New Reality

Ready for a boatload of fun

Laughter and joy

Second to none

Living Whole

The prize is won

Through your hard, deep Work

You have become

A Free Being

A Universal Citizen

Final Words

"What lies behind us and what lies before us are
tiny matters compared to what lies within us."

— Ralph Waldo Emerson

Resources

Helpguide.org—Free resources to help you resolve mental and emotional health issues. Includes hotlines and support groups. Helps you help yourself and others.

Children of Domestic Violence (cdv.org)

The Complete Empath Toolkit
by Michael R. Smith

The Emotion Code by Bradley Nelson

Emotional Freedom Technique (EFT)

Matt Kahn

John Newton

Tarek Bibi

Jeff Gignac

Sophia Zoe

Christine Day

Chief Golden Light Eagle

Andie DePass

Emmanuel Dagher

Tamra Oviatt

FoodBabe.com

Mercola.com

NaturalNews.com

Bioneers.org

WestonPrice.org

NextWorldTV.com

Cohousing.org

Findhorn.org

Crimes Against Nature
by Robert F. Kennedy

Cosmic Ordering Made Easier
by Ellen Watts

M. T. Keshe

Santos Bonacci

Dr. Masaru Emoto

Jean Houston

Vandana Shiva

Masanobu Fukuoka

Patty Greer

Chunyi Lin

Susun Weed

Tusli Gabbard

Paul Stamets

Buckmaster Fuller

David Wilcock

Lynn Waldrop

Janet Doerr

Karen LaGrange

Christel Hughes

Debora Wayne

Lanna Spencer

Jo Dunning

Lisa Transcendence Brown

Julie Renee

Eckhart Tolle

Neale Donald Walsch

Dorian Light

Lottie Cooper

Judy Cali

Marianne Williamson

Dr. Madlena Kantscheff

Dipal Shah

Peta Amber Lynn

Jarrad Hewett

Cathy Hohmeyer

Morry Zelcovitch

SARK

Shiloh Sophia

Aviva Gold

Ho'oponopono

Acim.org

Wopg.org

BirthingAndRebirthing.com

YouWealthRevolution.com

FromHeartacheToJoy.com

AcousticHealth.com

MagentaPixie.com

ScottWerner.org

GalacticConnection.com

ByDivineGrace.com

NotesFromTheUniverse.com

iands.org

TED Talks

Homeopathic Cell Salts

OptimumHealthInstitute.com

NewPhoenixRising.com

About The Author

After working many years in the public sector Nadja is reinventing herself as an artist and writer. She has an eclectic background. Her joys include adventuring on the Open Road, dancing, cooking, being in nature, writing and painting. She is also interested in natural building, organic gardening, alternative health, life-long learning, travel, and living moment to moment. Nadja writes for the conscious community and people who are interested in healing, meditation, transformation, ascension, and the New Earth. This includes highly sensitive people, Starseeds, Indigos, empaths, Light Workers, energy healers, artists, visionaries, and those in recovery and discovery.

Also By Nadja

Soft-cover books, eBooks, MP3s, and CDs
Smashwords, Amazon, Kindle, CreateSpace,
CDBaby, iTunes, YouTube, and your local
bookstore by request.

River of Living Light

Evolution Revolution

Random Thoughts and Poems

Hopi Blue Corn

El Maiz Azul de los Hopis

Visionary Tales for the New Earth

Color Me Bright Coloring Book

Blue Sky

Ascension Codes

Raps, Chants, and Rants

Women's Power Awakened

Ozzengoggle Poems

From the City of Shem

You Are Not Alone

Family Secrets

Flying Heart

Bullies